THE OFFICIAL
Sunderland afc
ANNUAL 2009

Written by Rob and Barbara Mason

This book belongs to

Age

Favourite player

Prediction of Sunderland's final position this season

Prediction of Barclays Premier League winners this season

Prediction of FA Cup winners this season

Prediction of Carling Cup winners this season

Prediction of teams to be relegated
from the Barclays Premier League this season:

18th

19th

20th

A TWOCAN PUBLICATION

©2008. Published by Twocan
under licence from Sunderland AFC

ISBN 978-0-9559299-0-8

PICTURE CREDITS
Getty Images, Blades Sports Photography, North News,
Twocan, Martin Walker and Rob Mason.

£6.99

THE OFFICIAL
Sunderland afc
ANNUAL 2009

CONTENTS

Sunderland is the first club Roy Keane has managed. Mr. Keane took over at the Stadium of Light on August 28th 2006. The first thing he did was bring in half a dozen players including Dwight Yorke to give Sunderland an injection of players used to winning matches. This was at a time when Sunderland had just been relegated with a record low number of points and had made a bad start to the new season.

ROY
Keane

The new manager got off to a great start winning his first two games both away from home and Sunderland went from strength to strength climbing from the foot of the table to the top as the Championship trophy was won with a handsome 5-0 away win at Luton.

Sunderland pipped Birmingham to the Championship trophy with the Blues winning promotion as runners up with Derby also promoted via the play offs. In the following 2007-08 season Keane inspired Sunderland to maintain Premier League status with two games to spare as Birmingham and Derby slid straight back down.

Determined to take Sunderland onwards and upwards to a new level amongst the clubs well established in the FA Barclays Premier League Roy spent the summer of 2008 attracting quality players to the Stadium of Light. The aim is to make Sunderland a club that are seen as a solid Premier League outfit who can hold their own in the top half of the table and be serious contenders in the cup competitions.

That is the next step for SAFC under Roy Keane. It may be easier said than done as the 3-0 home defeat to Manchester City at the end of August 2008 showed but Roy Keane never settled for anything but the best when he was a player and he isn't about to start accepting anything but high standards at Sunderland. Of course Roy Keane is one of the biggest names in world football. With him at the helm SAFC are aiming to get better and better with each passing season.

Sunderland AFC's
Player of the

Centre forward Kenwyne Jones is Sunderland's player of the year. He had to miss the start of the 2008-09 season because of an injury he received in the summer. Kenwyne was playing against England for Trinidad and Tobago. He was clean through and bearing down on goal when England goalie David James rushed out of goal in a desperate attempt to prevent a goal only for Kenwyne to be badly injured.

Jones' injury was a big blow to Sunderland as well as for Trinidad and Tobago. Since signing for Sunderland in August 2007 for £6m from Southampton Kenwyne has shown himself to be one of the best strikers in the Premier League.

England captain John Terry said Kenwyne was the best in the air in the Premier League after playing against him twice for Chelsea, Roy Keane said he wouldn't swap him for any other striker in the country and Sunderland supporters voted Jones their player of the season.

So what is it that makes Kenwyne Jones so good? Well for starters he is big and strong. Add to that the fact he is young and fast. Most importantly Kenwyne has the ability to jump really well and to time his jumps so that as the ball arrives he is at the peak of his jump. Time after time he climbs above the best defenders and can even compete with goalkeepers despite the advantage they have in being able to extend their arms in trying to reach the ball.

It's not just the goals Kenwyne scores but the goals he makes. Tables of Premier League 'assists' for his first season had him right up at the top of the tree alongside the likes of Steven Gerrard and Cesc Fabregas when it came to seeing which players had set up the most goals.

From the time he joined Sunderland, half the goals Sunderland scored in games Kenwyne played were either scored or made by him.

When he was just 21 he played in the last World Cup finals in Germany against England and Paraguay. It was the first time Trinidad and Tobago had qualified for the finals. Kenwyne also has experience of the Olympics having played in the 2004 Trinidad and Tobago team two years after representing his country in the FIFA U17 World Cup.

Kenwyne hasn't always been a striker. His international debut came in midfield and he has also impressed as a centre back but it as the main point of the attack that he is most valuable.

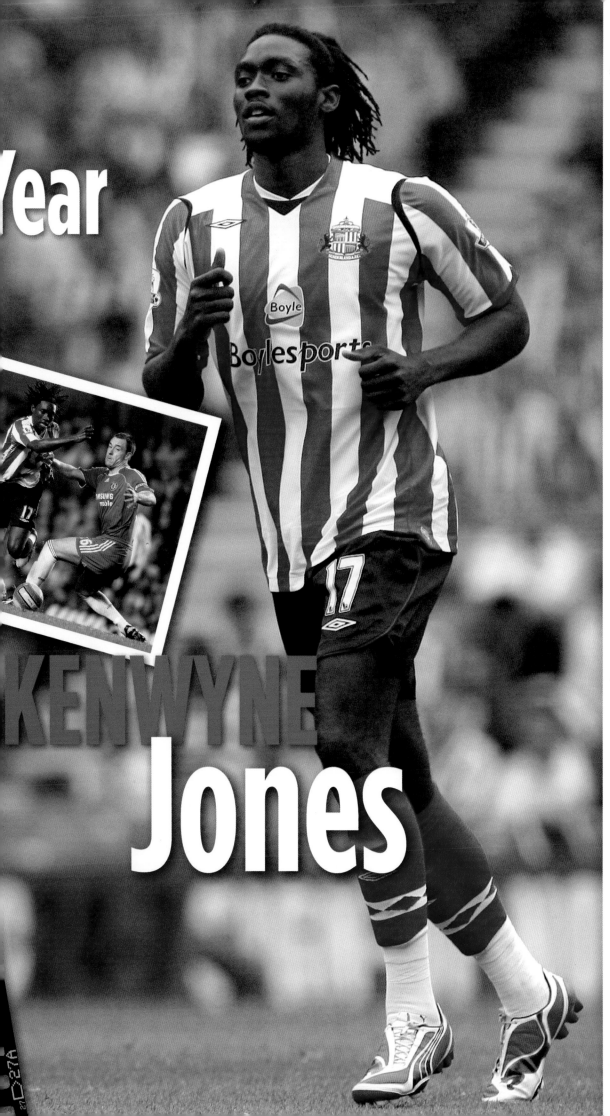

…Year

KENWYNE Jones

You would be hard pressed to find any Sunderland supporter who doesn't absolutely love Niall Quinn to bits.

He simply is fantastic in the eyes of Sunderland supporters. When he was a player at Sunderland Niall was once the club's record signing, costing £1.3m in 1996 as the club got ready for its first season in the Premier League.

He scored twice on his full debut but then had a lot of injury problems that meant by the time he was fully fit again he had to win the fans over.

Niall did this in spectacular fashion. When Kevin Phillips joined Sunderland hardly anyone had heard of the little striker bought from Watford but once Quinn and Phillips paired up it quickly became obvious this was a strike partnership made in heaven. Niall and Superkev looked like scoring every time they got the ball, Phillips became the top scorer not only in the Premier League but all of Europe and Niall weighed in with plenty of his own as well as being the Queen bee that Phillips buzzed around.

Sunderland supporters enjoy nothing more than beating local rivals Newcastle and The Mighty Quinn sealed his place in Sunderland supporters' affections by scoring not just in one win at Newcastle but in two successive 2-1 wins there in 1999 and 2000. Add to that the facts that Niall scored the first ever goal at the Stadium of Light and the first hat trick and throw in that during the glorious promotion season of 1998-99 when Sunderland achieved a record 105 points Niall scored the goal that beat eventual runners up Bradford on their own patch and then went in goal to keep a clean sheet and you have the sort of story even comic book writers would start to think might be stretching what was believable a bit too far.

Awarded a Benefit Match between Sunderland and his international team the Republic of Ireland (for whom at the time of his retirement he was the all time top scorer) Niall played part of the game for each team and raised £1m which he gave to hospitals in Sunderland and his home city Dublin as well as making a donation to a charity supporting Indian street children.

When injury forced Niall to hang up his boots, as a thank you to supporters Niall gave a brand new car to be given over in a competition in the match programme! All this would have been more than enough to ensure that at any time in the future Niall Quinn stepped foot back on Wearside the red and white carpet would be rolled out to welcome him back as true hero.

However all that is barely half the Niall Quinn Sunderland story. Niall had seen some great times as a Sunderland player, fantastic attacking displays in front of full stadiums such as the day Sunderland hammered Chelsea being 4-0 up after 38 minutes with Niall and Superkev scoring twice each. Quinny had also witnessed first hand the way the club responded to the massive disappointment of losing the most dramatic Play Off final ever on penalties in 1998 after a 4-4 draw with Charlton by winning more points than any team had ever done the following season.

After leaving the club though Niall had looked on as the best of times was replaced by the worst of times. Sunderland set a record low number of 19 Premier points as the team was relegated only to smash their own unwanted record just three years later. Not surprisingly given such demoralising seasons the supporters were losing the hope that had kept them going for so long even though those supporters kept loyally turning up week after week. It would have been easy for Niall to sit in the comfort of a TV studio as a pundit and talk about how sorry he was to see his old club in such a bad way.

Not Niall. He decided to act. The former centre forward made it his business to talk to his many contacts about what could be done to help the club. Having asked the former chairman if there was anything he could do to help he was surprised to be told that the best thing he could do was to see if he could actually buy the club. Undaunted Niall took advice from many of the influential people he knew and using his ability to communicate superbly with people persuaded a group of people who largely knew a lot about business and sport, but not necessarily football, to help provide financial backing to take over SAFC. A group called the Drumaville Consortium was created to allow Niall to take over the club.

To start with Niall became both chairman and manager until he could convince Roy Keane the time was right for Roy to start his managerial career. Niall only ever wanted to keep the managerial hot-seat warm and once Keane came in Quinn could concentrate on steering the club from the top.

Of course since Roy Keane took over the team have gone from strength to strength, winning the Championship, crucially managing to stay up in the always difficult first season after promotion and now given huge financial backing by Drumaville building a team to take Sunderland up the Barclays Premier League and to hopefully challenge for trophies.

COME ON WITHOUT COME ON WITHIN YOU'LL NOT SEE NOTHIN LIKE THE MIGHTY Quinn!

Niall himself would be the very last person to think he had achieved anything because as he keeps saying the moment you pat yourself on the back football has a way of kicking you and you'll be on the way back down.

For many Sunderland supporters though the main thing is not so much what Sunderland actually go on to achieve, it is the fact that under Niall's leadership Sunderland are thinking as big as their supporters have longed for them to do.

EL-HADJI
Diouf

DJIBRIL
Cisse

Test your knowledge of Sunderland's squad.

We have 38 questions for you about Roy Keane's players. For every one you get right you get three points as you do for a win. If you get a question partly right (for instance if you get one of the players in question 7) you get one point as you do for a draw and obviously if you are wrong or don't know the answer you get nothing as you do for a defeat.

When you've totalled up your points see the league table for last season and work out where you would have finished.

Good luck.

How high can you go?

PREMIER LEAGUE 2007·2008

	P	W	D	L	F	A	W	D	L	F	A	GD	P
Man Utd	38	17	1	1	47	7	10	5	4	33	15	+58	87
Chelsea	38	12	7	0	36	13	13	3	3	29	13	+39	85
Arsenal	38	14	5	0	37	11	10	6	3	37	20	+43	83
Liverpool	38	12	6	1	43	13	9	7	3	24	15	+39	76
Everton	38	11	4	4	34	17	8	4	7	21	16	+22	65
Aston Villa	38	10	3	6	34	22	6	9	4	37	29	+20	60
Blackburn	38	8	7	4	26	19	7	6	6	24	29	+2	58
Portsmouth	38	7	8	4	24	14	9	1	9	24	26	+8	57
Man City	38	11	4	4	28	20	4	6	9	17	33	-8	55
West Ham	38	7	7	5	24	24	6	3	10	18	26	-8	49
Spurs	38	8	5	6	46	34	3	8	8	20	27	+5	46
Newcastle	38	8	5	6	25	26	3	5	11	20	39	-20	43
Boro	38	7	5	7	27	23	3	7	9	16	30	-10	42
Wigan	38	8	5	6	21	17	2	5	12	13	34	-17	40
Sunderland	**38**	**9**	**3**	**7**	**23**	**21**	**2**	**3**	**14**	**13**	**38**	**-23**	**39**
Bolton	38	7	5	7	23	18	2	5	12	13	36	-18	37
Fulham	38	5	5	9	22	31	3	7	9	16	29	-22	36
Reading	38	8	2	9	19	25	2	4	13	22	41	-25	36
Birmingham	38	6	8	5	30	23	2	3	14	16	39	-16	35
Derby	38	1	5	13	12	43	0	3	16	8	46	-69	11

The answers are on page 62.

All the questions relate to Sunderland's squad as the transfer window closed at the end of August 2008.

All the answers to the questions are to be found in the player profiles beginning on page 22 of your annual.

01 Which Sunderland player is a lifelong friend of the rap star Akon?

02 Which member of Roy Keane's squad scored a penalty for Liverpool in the 2005 Champions League final?

03 Name the player who won BBC TV's Goal of the Month in February 2008 with a brilliant shot against Wigan?

04 Who is the Sunderland born player who made his league debut when on loan to Rotherham?

05 Which defender once played in the UEFA Cup for Glasgow Rangers?

06 Who is the Sunderland player who has played international cricket?

07 Which two players were named Joint north east players of the year for 2007.

08 Who joined Sunderland from West Ham in August 2008?

09 Craig Gordon helped Hearts win the 2006 Scottish Cup final on penalties against which team that no longer exist?

10 Which striker scored twice at the Stadium of Light for England U20s in 2002?

11 Which striker was the top scorer in Europe in the qualifying games for Euro 2008?

12 Which member of the squad's previous clubs are Mansfield, Notts County, Nottingham Forest and Norwich City?

13 Which country does El-Hadji Diouf play for?

14 Who played in the League Cup finals of 2008 and 2006?

19 Teemu Tainio plays for which country?

20 Who scored twice on his England debut?

21 Keeper Nick Colgan is an international for which country?

22 South Shields born young striker who made his debut against Man Utd on Boxing Day 2007?

23 Name the Sunderland player who has twice been African Player of the Year.

24 Which Sunderland player has a stadium named after him?

25 This player has played for Man Utd, Port Vale, Preston, Norwich, Leeds and Fulham. Who is it?

26 Phil Bardsley, Kieran Richardson and Paul McShane were team mates in a Man Utd team that won the FA Youth Cup in which year?

27 What do Ross Wallace, Russell Anderson, Greg Halford, Arnau, Trevor Carson and Roy O'Donovan have in common this season?

28 Which player lists his previous clubs as: Le Havre, Bastia, Wigan and Spurs?

29 Which defender was born on August 6th 1980 in Chester?

30 Who is the player who scored in the 2006 FA Cup final for Liverpool?

31 Steed Malbranque has represented France at U21 level but which country was he born in?

15 Which player was given his international debut by Sunderland's 1973 FA Cup final goalscorer Ian Porterfield?

16 Patrice Carteron and Christian Bassila have both played for Sunderland. Which member of Ropy Keane's squad was their team mate when they were at Lyon?

17 Which three Sunderland players have played for Nottingham Forest?

18 Apart from Sunderland which club have Kenwyne Jones, Daryl Murphy and Graham Kavanagh all played for?

32 Which player was signed from Gillingham?

33 Who is the oldest member of the squad?

34 Which player made his Premier League debut against Sunderland for Man Utd?

35 Which player started at a club called Joe Public?

36 Who was the League of Ireland Young Player of the Year in 2004?

37 Who was captain of Charlton before joining Sunderland?

38 Name the five squad members who have played in the World Cup finals.

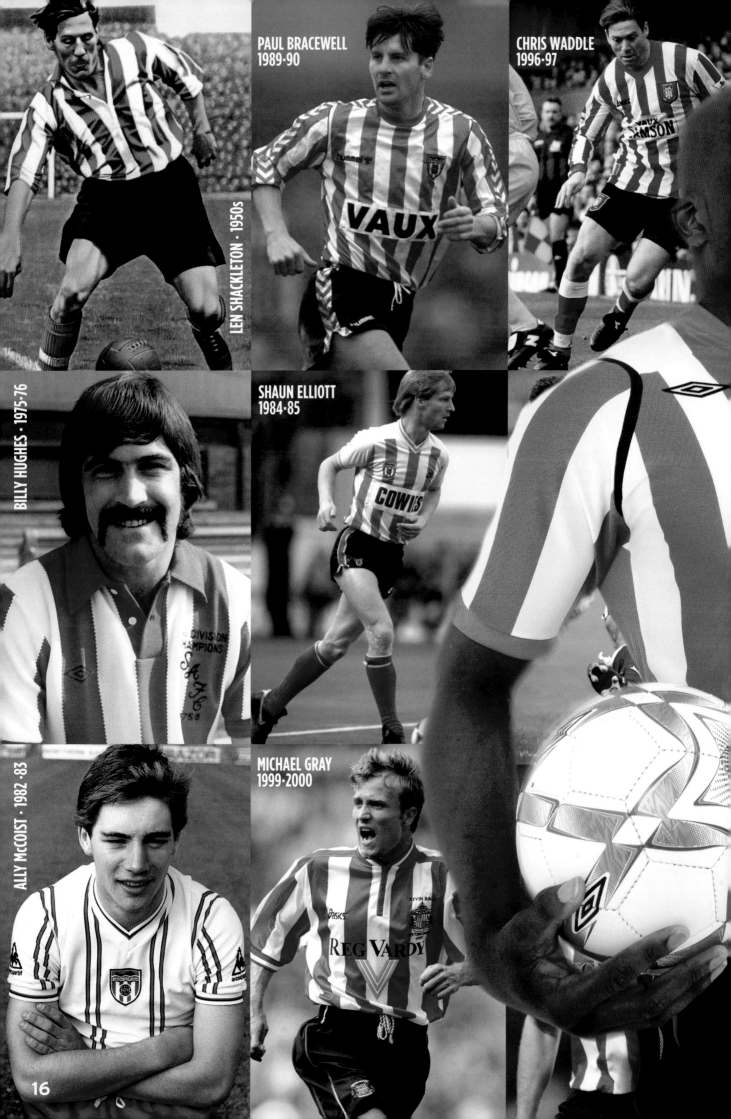

LEN SHACKLETON · 1950s

PAUL BRACEWELL
1989-90

CHRIS WADDLE
1996-97

BILLY HUGHES · 1975-76

SHAUN ELLIOTT
1984-85

ALLY McCOIST · 1982-83

MICHAEL GRAY
1999-2000

think of Sunderland and you think of red and white stripes. There are other teams who play in red and white stripes of course – how many can you think of? There are five other teams in England in either the Premier League or Football League but if you add up all the league titles, FA Cups or League Cups those five have won their combined total comes to less than what Sunderland have achieved.

In Spain Athletic Bilbao also wear red and white stripes. They do this because they were formed by a man from Sunderland - Arthur Pentland - and so began wearing red and white stripes, something they still proudly do.

Sunderland were formed in 1879. To begin with Sunderland actually wore blue kits before switching to red and white but initially in halved shirts like Blackburn's are now only in red and white. Sunderland didn't wear red and white stripes until 1887-88 but ever since then that has been the Lads' colours.

In the early 1980s Sunderland had a couple of years where they wore a mainly white shirt with thin red and white stripes. This kit was made by Le Coq Sportif and was widely hated by Sunderland fans who mainly insisted on still wearing traditional red and white stripes which were quickly brought back

rather than a kit the fans thought looked like a set of pyjamas.

These days Sunderland's strips are made by Umbro, one of the world's top sportswear manufacturers. For the 2008-09 season the socks returned to red after a few years of wearing black socks. Sunderland's shorts are traditionally black although throughout most of the 1960s Sunderland wore white shorts, changing back to black in 1972 in Bob Stokoe's first match in charge - it was just the first of the great things Stokoe did as six months later he brought the FA Cup to Sunderland.

Had he kept the white shorts there would have been a colour clash of shorts with Leeds in the cup final – he must have known!

KEVIN BALL
1995-96

ALLAN
JOHNSTON
1997-98

NYRON
NOSWORTHY
2008-09

THE FAMOUS
Red & White
STRIPES

Stadium o

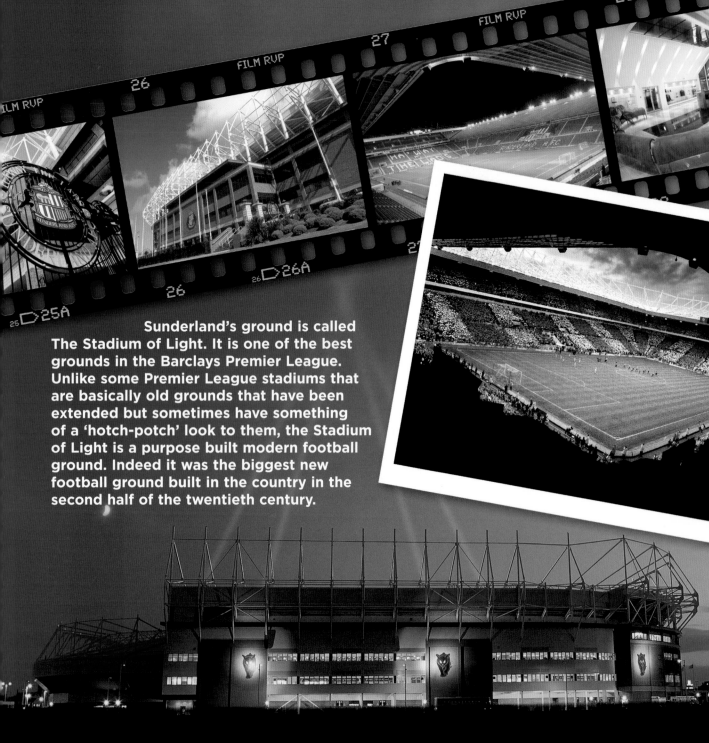

Sunderland's ground is called The Stadium of Light. It is one of the best grounds in the Barclays Premier League. Unlike some Premier League stadiums that are basically old grounds that have been extended but sometimes have something of a 'hotch-potch' look to them, the Stadium of Light is a purpose built modern football ground. Indeed it was the biggest new football ground built in the country in the second half of the twentieth century.

LET THERE BE LIGHT!

Light

Built in 1997 the Stadium of Light at first could hold 42,000 fans but because Sunderland were regularly filling it the ground was extended in 2001 when the north stand of the ground had an extra level added to it to take the capacity up to 49,000. Built by the same company who constructed Ajax's Amsterdam ArenA, the Stadium of Light was designed in such a way that should Sunderland wish to further develop areas of the ground they can easily do so as has already happened with the North Stand.

As well as having one of the finest stadiums in the country, Sunderland also have a training ground that is absolutely first class. The Academy of Light is two and a half miles away from the Stadium of Light. It is a huge complex with many football pitches, excellent gym facilities, swimming pools and media areas. The academy also has its own wetland areas that offer a haven for wildlife and store water that is used to irrigate the pitches as SAFC take their environmental responsibilities very seriously.

With clubs like Everton and Liverpool looking to build new grounds and Arsenal having a superb new stadium but at massive cost, Sunderland – with a top class modern ground and training base already in place – can concentrate now entirely on football and continuing to build a team to grace the Stadium of Light.

WHY IS THE GROUND CALLED THE STADIUM OF LIGHT?

Sunderland's ground has an unusual name. Some clubs call their stadiums after their sponsors but that has not been the case at The Stadium of Light. Some people think that for some strange reason Sunderland called their ground after Benfica's Stadium of Light in Portugal but that is not true. Benfica's stadium is named after the area of Lisbon the ground is in which is called Luz (meaning Light in Portuguese).

Look outside Sunderland's Stadium of Light and you will find a permanently lit monument of a miners' lamp. The ground is built on what used to be Monkwearmouth Colliery, the biggest coal mine in the Durham coalfield. Miners wore helmets with lights attached to them to help them find their way underground. Calling the ground the Stadium of Light is a way of honouring all those people who before the football ground was there toiled underground.

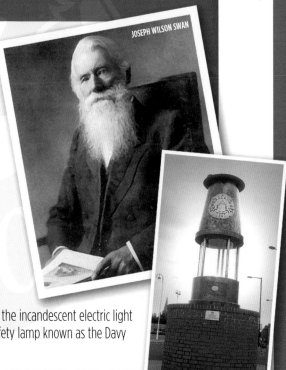

JOSEPH WILSON SWAN

Another reason for calling the ground The Stadium of Light is that the inventor of the incandescent electric light Joseph Wilson Swan was born in Sunderland while the inventor of the miners' safety lamp known as the Davy Lamp was invented by Sir Humphrey Davy in the Durham coalfield.

VIC HALOM · 1972-73

PHIL GRAY · 1994-95

PAUL BRACEWELL · 1995-96

ERIC GATES · 1989-90

CRAIG RUSSELL · 1996-97

JOHN BYRNE · 1991-92

KEVIN PHILLIPS
1998-1999

JULIO ARCA · 2005-06

20

Away
THE LADS

**KEVIN PHILLPS
1996-97**

**DEAN
WHITEHEAD
2006-07**

**KENWYNE
JONES
2008-09**

Sunderland are wearing an Umbro two tone blue striped shirt as their away kit this season. Over the years Sunderland have often worn blue kits of one shade or another as their away kit although at times yellow, white, mustard and even very dark blue/black have been used. Given that blue was the club's original colour there is always a clear historical link with Sunderland donning blue as they do this season.

In the very first match at the Stadium of Light in 1997 against Ajax Sunderland wore their traditional red and white striped home kit in the first half but ran out for the second half modelling the brand new away kit which was being revealed. It was a mustard colour that fans didn't like and come the end of the season it brought tears to their eyes when Michael Gray's fateful play off final penalty shoot out kick was saved. Pictures of Michael looking shell-shocked at the miss in that away kick remain the best known pictures of that kit.

In 1994-95 Sunderland wore a greeny blue kit officially called Teale. This was produced by a company called Avec. The shorts featured a large red triangle on both the front and back. Most supporters disliked this kit especially because of the shorts but as always choice of kit is a matter of personal taste. Take a look at the away kits Sunderland have worn that are shown here and decide which one you think are the best and the worst.

Goalkeeper

BORN: December 31st 1982, Edinburgh.

FORMER CLUBS: Hearts

SQUAD NUMBER: 1

FIVE FACTS ABOUT CRAIG:

Craig is the most expensive 'keeper in Britain after costing a reported £9m.

He helped Hearts win the Scottish Cup in 2006 beating Gretna on penalties.

He watched the 2002 Champions League final between Real Madrid and Bayer Leverkusen at Hampden Park.

Made his Scotland debut in 2004 against Trinidad & Tobago who included Carlos Edwards.

Craig likes Kanye West, Black Eyed Peas and Michael Jackson.

NICK
COLGAN

BORN: September 19th 1973, Drogheda.

SQUAD NUMBER: 46

FORMER CLUBS: Drogheda, Chelsea, Bournemouth, Hibs, Barnsley and Ipswich plus loans to Crewe, Grimsby, Millwall, Brentford, Reading, Stockport & Dundee Utd.

FIVE FACTS ABOUT NICK:

Nick is a full ROI international.

Sunderland were the FA Cup holders when Nick was born.

Although Nick had been on the books of 13 clubs before joining Sunderland, all but 28 of his 282 club appearances were for Hibs or Barnsley.

He helped Barnsley to play off success on penalties in 2006.

Nick has a one year contract at SAFC.

MARTON
FULOP

BORN: May 3rd 1983, Budapest.

SQUAD NUMBER: 32

FORMER CLUBS: MTK, Elore, Bodaj (all Hungary), Spurs, Chesterfield (loan), Coventry (loan) Stoke (loan).

FIVE FACTS ABOUT MARTON:

Marton is a full Hungary international.

Given his appetite his team mates nickname Marton 'Never' ...and he's from Hungary.

Marton nearly signed for Stoke at the start of this season.

His Premier League debut came in the final match of last season.

Marton was the first ever player to be transferred from Spurs to Sunderland.

DARREN

BORN: 11th May 1974, Worksop.

SQUAD NUMBER: 13

FORMER CLUBS:
Mansfield,
Notts County,
Nottingham Forest,
Norwich City.

FIVE FACTS ABOUT DARREN:

Darren is a full Wales international.

He is the quiz master of the 'Daz Challenge' – the players' trivia quiz in SAFC's match programme.

At the start of this season Darren had made 489 league appearances.

He won a Championship medal with Sunderland in 2007.

He made his league debut with Mansfield in 1992-93

TREVOR
CARSON

BORN: March 5th 1988, Downpatrick.

SQUAD NUMBER: 24

FORMER CLUBS: None

FIVE FACTS ABOUT TREVOR:

Trevor is on loan to Chesterfield this season.

He is a Northern Ireland U21 international.

When he was in the U18s he occasionally played as a striker.

He captained the reserves in 2008 when Sunderland won the Durham Challenge Cup.

Yet to make his first team debut for SAFC he has been on the bench several times.

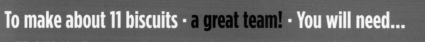

To make about 11 biscuits · a great team! · You will need...

- 325g Self Raising flour
- 100g caster sugar
- black, red and white writing icing

- pinch salt
- 50g margarine
- 3 tblsp milk

- 3 tsp ground ginger
- 3 tblsp golden syrup
- 250g white ready to roll icing sugar

You will also need a clean mixing bowl, saucepan and rolling pin, 3 large flat baking trays, a piece of stiff card to make a template, a sharp knife and a cooling tray.

STEP 6

WHAT YOU WILL NEED

STEP 4

Samson shows you how to make gingerbread cat biscui ...a purrfect treat

1. Wash your paws, turn on the oven to 160°C, 325°f, gas 3. Grease the baking trays with a little margarine.

2. Place the flour, salt and ginger in a bowl and mix together

3. Warm the sugar, margarine and syrup in a pan until melted.

4. Add this mixture to the flour and stir together, add the milk and mix until it all sticks together in a sticky ball.

5. Scatter plenty of flour on a clean work surface and on your rolling pin to stop the mixture from sticking.

6. Roll the mixture out flat until it is about 1 cm thick.

7. Trace the template onto the card and cut out the shape.

8. Lay this shape on the mixture and cut out using a sharp knife.

9. Place on the baking trays well spaced out.

10. Bake in the oven for approximately 10-15 minutes.

11. Allow to cool slightly before carefully lifting off onto a cooling tray then leave until cold hardened.

12. Roll out the white icing, then cut a shirt shape using your template (left) guide and place one on each biscuit using a few drops of water to make

13. Using the writing icing to put stripes on the shirts, a red nose and mouth and finish the eyes.

14. Leave to set before eating.

24

Samson's Biscuit Making

DON'T EAT THEM ALL IN ONE GO!

25

PHIL BARDSLEY

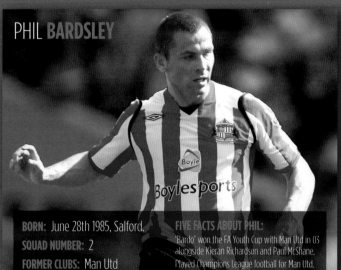

BORN: June 28th 1985, Salford.

SQUAD NUMBER: 2

FORMER CLUBS: Man Utd plus loans to Antwerp, Burnley, Glasgow Rangers, Aston Villa and Sheffield United.

FIVE FACTS ABOUT PHIL:
'Bardo' won the FA Youth Cup with Man Utd in 03 alongside Kieran Richardson and Paul McShane.
Played Champions League football for Man Utd.
Played in the UEFA Cup for Rangers.
Likes Rod Stewart, Oasis and Arctic Monkeys.
Made his full Premier League debut against Sunderland for Man Utd. in 2005-06.

PASCAL CHIMBONDA

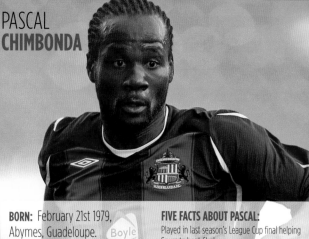

BORN: February 21st 1979, Abymes, Guadeloupe.

SQUAD NUMBER: 21

FORMER CLUBS: Le Havre, Bastia (both France), Wigan Athletic, Tottenham Hotspur.

FIVE FACTS ABOUT PASCAL:
Played in last season's League Cup final helping Spurs to beat Chelsea.
Played in the 2006 League Cup final for Wigan.
Has been capped by France.
Played UEFA Cup football for Spurs.
Made his third appearance in English football against Sunderland for Wigan in 2005.

DANNY COLLINS

BORN: August 6th 1980, Chester

SQUAD NUMBER: 15

FORMER CLUBS: Buckley Town, Chester, Vauxhall Motors (loan)

FIVE FACTS ABOUT DANNY:
As a schoolboy Dan was a team-mate of Michael Owen with Deeside boys.
Capped at both cricket & football by Wales.
He has also been capped at football by the England non league team.
When with non league Vauxhall Motors Dan helped to knock QPR out of the FA Cup.
Had played only 4 Football League games when playing SAFC at the SoL in the League Cup in 04.

ANTON FERDINAND

BORN: February 18th 1985

SQUAD NUMBER: 26

FORMER CLUBS: West Ham United

FIVE FACTS ABOUT ANTON:
He made his West Ham debut on the opening day of the 2003-04 season.
He grew up with Kieran Richardson who was also at West Ham as a youngster.
He debuted for England U21s at Middlesbrough in 2004.
He scored in West Ham wins over Man Utd and Fulham in 2007-08.
He played over 160 games for his first club.

GEORGE McCARTNEY

BORN: April 29th 1981, Belfast

SQUAD NUMBER: 3

FORMER CLUBS: West Ham

FIVE FACTS ABOUT GEORGE:
George was developed as an Academy player at Sunderland.
He was transferred from Sunderland to West Ham in 2006.
He returned to Sunderland in September 2008.
George is a Northern Ireland international.
He was Sunderland's Player of the year in 2004-05.

PAUL McSHANE

BORN: January 6th 1986, Wicklow.

SQUAD NUMBER: 30

FORMER CLUBS: Man Utd, Walsall (loan), Brighton (loan) WBA.

FIVE FACTS ABOUT PAUL:
Scored on league debut on Boxing Day 2004 against Sheffield Wed. while on loan to Walsall.
Was Brighton's Player of the Year while on a season long loan.
Man of the Match on full international debut for the Republic of Ireland V Czech Republic in 2006.
Is on a season long loan to Hull City
Paul's dad played Hurling for Dublin.

BORN: October 11th 1980, Brixton.

FORMER CLUBS: Gillingham

SQUAD NUMBER: 5

FIVE FACTS ABOUT NYRON:

Was North East Player of the Year in 2007 jointly with Dean Whitehead.

Sometimes played up front for Gillingham, once scoring twice in a local derby with Crystal Palace.

Won a Championship medal with Sunderland in 2007.

Was converted from a right back to a centre back by Roy Keane.

During last season Nyron was named as the country's top defender by the Actim Index.

Defenders

Nyron Nosworthy

Samson's Shout

| HOME | NEWS | COMMERCIAL | TICKETS | STORE |

Hi June,

Question-time for Carlos

Samson and Delilah caught up with Carlos Edwards on his return from Portugal.

More

Five minutes with... Jamie Chandler

Jamie Chandler chats about his busy summer on England duty, as well as his hopes for this season at Sunderland.

Read on

24-7 is Sunderland's junior supporters club. It is called 24-7 because Sunderland fans support their team 24 hours a day, 7 days a week. Any young Sunderland supporter up the age of 16 can join 24-7 and really you'd be mad not to ...BECAUSE IT'S FREE!

If you live in England, Scotland, Wales, Northern Ireland or the Republic of Ireland joining 24-7 costs you absolutely nothing, nowt, zilch, nil...and we hope we aren't saying nil when talking about Sunderland too often!

If you live outside those countries joining 24-7 costs you £5 towards international posting costs.

24-7 members have SAFC 24-7 poster magazines sent to them so they can show they are part of the red and white family. Members also receive a 24-7 membership card and receive a monthly email from Sunderland's mascot Samson as well has having their own special section of the club's website safc.com devoted to them.

SAFC 24-7 is the place for all young Sunderland supporte **If you haven't signed for Sunderland yet, what are you waiting fo**

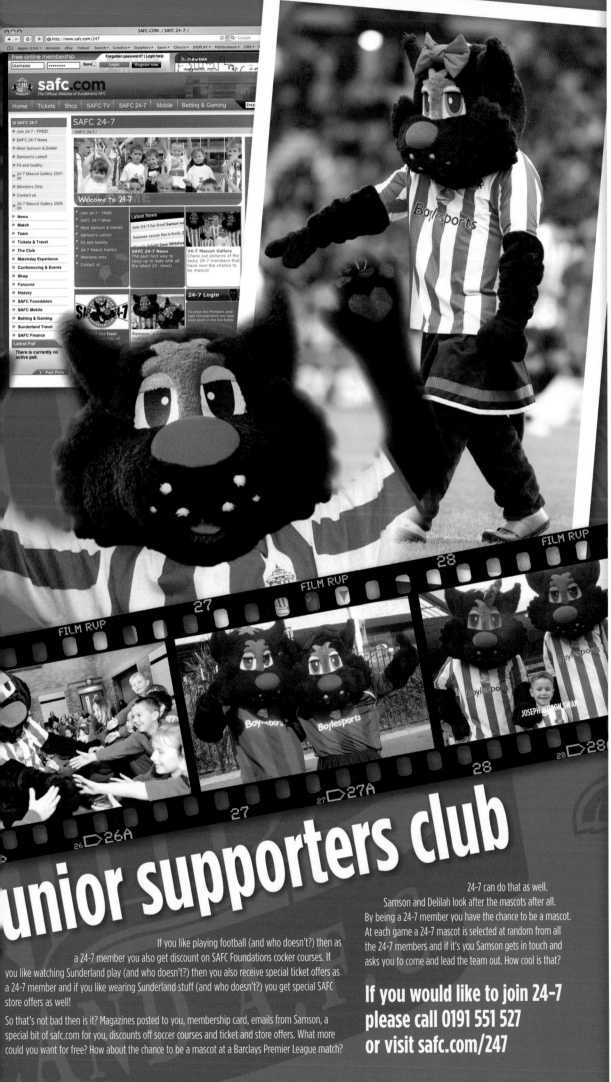

unior supporters club

24-7 can do that as well.
Samson and Delilah look after the mascots after all.
By being a 24-7 member you have the chance to be a mascot.
At each game a 24-7 mascot is selected at random from all
the 24-7 members and if it's you Samson gets in touch and
asks you to come and lead the team out. How cool is that?

If you like playing football (and who doesn't?) then as
a 24-7 member you also get discount on SAFC Foundations cocker courses. If
you like watching Sunderland play (and who doesn't?) then you also receive special ticket offers as
a 24-7 member and if you like wearing Sunderland stuff (and who doesn't?) you get special SAFC
store offers as well!

So that's not bad then is it? Magazines posted to you, membership card, emails from Samson, a
special bit of safc.com for you, discounts off soccer courses and ticket and store offers. What more
could you want for free? How about the chance to be a mascot at a Barclays Premier League match?

**If you would like to join 24-7
please call 0191 551 527
or visit safc.com/247**

EL-HADJI DIOUF

BORN: January 15th 1981, Dakar, Senegal, Africa.

SQUAD NUMBER: 11

FORMER CLUBS: Sochaux, Rennes, Lens (all France), Liverpool, Bolton Wanderers.

FIVE FACTS ABOUT EL-HADJI:
El-Hadji has twice been African Footballer of the Year.
Won the League Cup with Liverpool in 2003, playing against Roy Keane and Man Utd.
Played five games in the 2002 World Cup finals.
Scored a hat trick for Senegal against Namibia in a World Cup qualifying game in 2001.
Is a lifelong friend of rap star Akon.

GRAHAM KAVANAGH

BORN: December 2nd 1973

SQUAD NUMBER: 28

FORMER CLUBS: Home Farm, Middlesbrough, Darlington (loan), Stoke City, Cardiff City, Wigan Athletic, Sheffield Wednesday (loan).

FIVE FACTS ABOUT GRAHAM:
Kav is a Republic of Ireland international.
Twice reached double figures in a season for league goals.
One of six players signed by Roy Keane within a day or two of him becoming SAFC manager.
Played with Chimbonda in 2006 L.Cup final for Wigan.
Kav was a promotion winner with Cardiff in 2003.

GRANT LEADBITTER

BORN: January 7th 1986, Sunderland.

SQUAD NUMBER: 18

FORMER CLUBS: Rotherham (loan)

FIVE FACTS ABOUT GRANT:
Grant is an England U21 international.
Sunderland born Mick Harford gave Grant his league debut when he was on loan at Rotherham United.
He is a product of the Sunderland academy.
He was third top scorer with seven goals in the 2006-07 promotion season.
Grant wears no 18 because he admires Paul Scholes who wears the same number.

LIAM MILLER

BORN: February 13th 1981, Cork.

SQUAD NUMBER: 12

FORMER CLUBS: Celtic, Aarhus (Denmark - loan), Manchester United, Leeds United (Loan)

FIVE FACTS ABOUT LIAM:
Liam is a Republic of Ireland international.
He scored his first goal for Sunderland on his second appearance, back at his old club Leeds.
Joined just after Roy Keane became manager.
Won a Championship medal in his first year on Wearside.
His first goal at the Stadium of Light was a dramatic injury time header in a crucial promotion clash with Derby in 2007.

STEED MALBRANQUE

BORN: January 6th 1980, Mouscron, Belgium

SQUAD NUMBER: 8

FORMER CLUBS: Olympique Lyonnais (France), Fulham, Spurs.

FIVE FACTS ABOUT STEED:
In the Spurs League Cup winning team of 2008.
Played for France in the European Under 21 championship in 2002.
Scored twice for Fulham in a 4-1 win at Newcastle.
Played in the Champions League for Lyon.
At Lyon his team mates included Patrice Carteron & Christian Bassila who both later played for SAFC.

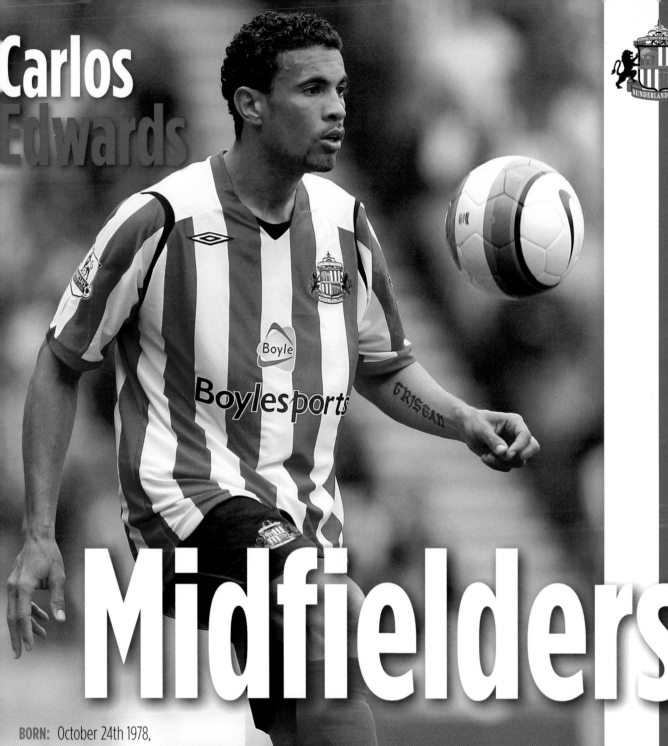

Carlos Edwards

Midfielders

BORN: October 24th 1978, Port of Spain, Trinidad.

FORMER CLUBS: Queens Park Rangers (of Trinidad, not England), Defence Force (Trinidad), Wrexham, Luton Town.

SQUAD NUMBER: 7

FIVE FACTS ABOUT CARLOS:

Played for former Sunderland manager Denis Smith at Wrexham.

Played for SAFC's 1973 FA Cup final goalscorer Ian Porterfield for Trinidad and Tobago.

Won the LDV trophy at the Millennium Stadium in 2005 with Wrexham.

Played in the 2006 World Cup.

Won the league in Trinidad with Defence Force in 1999.

ANDY REID

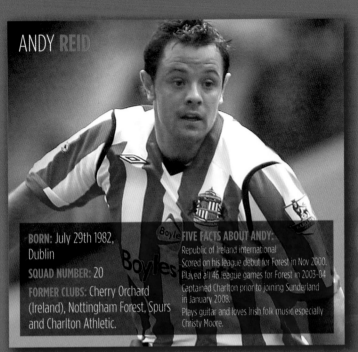

BORN: July 29th 1982, Dublin

SQUAD NUMBER: 20

FORMER CLUBS: Cherry Orchard (Ireland), Nottingham Forest, Spurs and Charlton Athletic.

FIVE FACTS ABOUT ANDY:
Republic of Ireland international
Scored on his league debut for Forest in Nov 2000.
Played all 46 league games for Forest in 2003-04
Captained Charlton prior to joining Sunderland in January 2008.
Plays guitar and loves Irish folk music especially Christy Moore.

KIERAN RICHARDSON

BORN: October 21st 1984, Greenwich.

SQUAD NUMBER: 20

FORMER CLUBS: West Ham, Man Utd, West Bromwich Albion (loan).

FIVE FACTS ABOUT PASCAL:
Scored twice on his England debut v USA in 2005.
Won a League Cup winner's medal in 2006 for Manchester Utd against a Wigan team including Chimbonda and Kavanagh.
Scored in the Champions League for Man Utd.
Scored on WBA debut in 2005 and played a major role in keeping them up.
Was with West Ham as a youngster but won the FA Youth Cup with Man Utd.

TEEMU TAINIO

BORN: November 27th 1979, Tornio, Finland.

SQUAD NUMBER: 4

FORMER CLUBS: Haka (Finland), Auxerre (France), Tottenham Hotspur.

FIVE FACTS ABOUT TEEMU:
Finland international.
Played Champions League football for Auxerre.
Played in the UEFA Cup for Auxerre and Spurs.
One of three players to move from Spurs to SAFC after winning the League Cup in 2008.
Scored in the French Cup semi final in 2005 for Auxerre v Nimes.

DWIGHT YORKE

BORN: November 3rd 1971, Canaan, Tobago

SQUAD NUMBER: 19

FORMER CLUBS: St Clair's (Tobago), Aston Villa, Man Utd., Blackburn Rovers, Birmingham City, Sydney.

FIVE FACTS ABOUT DWIGHT:
Has a stadium named after him in Trinidad & Tobago
Is great friends with legendary West Indian batsman Brian Lara.
Won the Champions League with Man Utd.
Played in the 2006 World Cup.
Was playing in Australia when Roy Keane persuaded him to come back and play for SAFC

DEAN WHITEHEAD

BORN: January 12th 1982, Oxford

SQUAD NUMBER: 6

FORMER CLUBS: Oxford United

FIVE FACTS ABOUT DEAN:
Joint North East Footballer of the Year for 2007 with Nyron Nosworthy.
Captained Sunderland to the Championship in 2007.
Turned down Coventry to sign for home town team Oxford as a boy.
Played for former Sunderland manager Denis Smith at Oxford.
Oxford's Player of the Year and in the PFA D3 team of the year in 2004.

DELILAH'S PICTURE Quiz

WHO AM I?

We've disguised three SAFC stars. Can you identity them?

A   B   C

SPOT THE DIFFERENCE

There are eight differences between these two pictures of Pascal Chimbonda.

Answers on page 62.

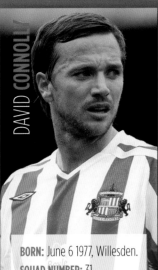

DAVID CONNOLLY

BORN: June 6 1977, Willesden.

SQUAD NUMBER: 31

FORMER CLUBS: Watford, Feyenoord (Holland), Excelsior (Loan – Holland), Wolves, Wimbledon, West Ham, Leicester and Wigan.

FIVE FACTS ABOUT DAVID:

David is a Republic of Ireland international.

At the start of this season he had 41 international caps and nine goals.

He was top scorer for Sunderland in the Championship winning 2006-07 season.

He scored 29 goals in 32 games for Excelsior in Holland in 1999-2000

In 2002-03 he scored 24 goals in 28 games for Wimbledon.

MICHAEL KILOPPA

BORN: December 23rd 1983, Newcastle.

SQUAD NUMBER: 16

FORMER CLUBS: Newcastle, Watford (loan), Nottingham Forest (loan), Barnsley (loan), Cardiff.

FIVE FACTS ABOUT MICHAEL:

England U21 international.

Scored twice for England U20s against Italy U20s at the Stadium of Light in 2002.

Scored four times in a 7-4 win over Burnley while with Watford.

Second top scorer in the Championship with 22 goals for Cardiff (including two at the Stadium of Light) in 2006-07.

Scored last minute winner v. Spurs on Sunderland debut in 2007.

DJIBRIL CISSE

BORN: August 12th 1981, Arles, France.

SQUAD NUMBER: 9

FORMER CLUBS: Auxerre (France), Liverpool, Marseille (France)

FIVE FACTS ABOUT DJIBRIL:

Djibril scored in the Champions League final penalty shoot out for Liverpool when they beat A.C. Milan in 2005.

He scored in the 2006 FA Cup final for Liverpool against West Ham.

He scored twice in the French Cup final in 2007 and also in the 2003 French Cup final.

He is the Lord of Frodsham, a title he obtained when buying his home in Cheshire.

Scored on his SAFC debut at Spurs in August 2008.

DAV HEA

BORN: August 5th 1979, Downpatrick.

SQUAD NUMBER: 23

FORMER CLUBS: Man Utd, Por Vale (loan), Preston, Norwich (loan), Leeds and Fulham.

FIVE FACTS ABOUT DAVID:

Northern Ireland international.

Was the top scorer in Europe in qualification games for Euro 08.

Scored a brilliant goal against Sunderland for Fulham in April 2008.

Scored on his Sunderland debut at Nottingham Forest in August 2008.

Comes from the same place as young Sunderland 'keeper Trevor Carson.

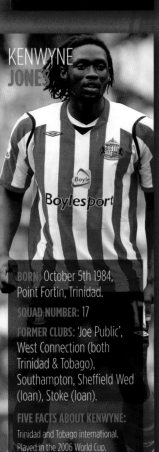

KENWYNE JONES

BORN: October 5th 1984, Point Fortin, Trinidad.

SQUAD NUMBER: 17

FORMER CLUBS: 'Joe Public', West Connection (both Trinidad & Tobago), Southampton, Sheffield Wed (loan), Stoke (loan).

FIVE FACTS ABOUT KENWYNE:

Trinidad and Tobago international.

Played in the 2006 World Cup.

Originally a centre back.

Top scorer and Player of the year at Sunderland in 2007-08

Once scored seven goals in seven games on loan to Sheffield Wednesday.

RADE PRICA

BORN: June 30th 1980, Ljungby, Sweden.

SQUAD NUMBER: 45

FORMER CLUBS: Ljungby, Helsingborg (both Sweden), Hansa Rostock (Germany), Aalborg (Denmark).

FIVE FACTS ABOUT RADE:

Sweden international

Joint top scorer in Danish league in 2006-07.

Scored on Sunderland debut v Birmingham in January 2008.

Won Swedish league championship with Helsingborg in 1999.

Champions League experience included a win over Inter Milan for Helsingborg.

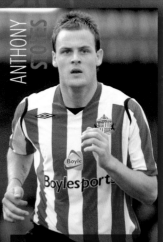

ANTHONY STOKES

BORN: July 25th 1988, Dublin.

SQUAD NUMBER: 44

FORMER CLUBS: Arsenal, Falkirk (loan)

FIVE FACTS ABOUT ANTHONY:

Republic of Ireland international.

Scored 14 goals in 16 Scottish Premier League appearances while on loan to Falkirk.

Made Arsenal debut at Sunderland as a substitute in a League cup tie.

Scored hat tricks in consecutive games for Falkirk in the Autumn of 2006.

Scored his first Sunderland goal at Plymouth in February 2007.

MARTYN WAGHO

BORN: January 23rd 1990, South Shields.

SQUAD NUMBER: 39

FORMER CLUBS: None

FIVE FACTS ABOUT MARTYN:

Made his first team debut against Manchester Utd on Boxing Day 2007.

Won the Man of the Match award on his debut.

Played in the 2007 FA Youth Cup semi final against Manchester City.

Scored 21 goals in 21 starts plus 5 sub appearances for the Academy U18s in 2007-08

Scored a FA Youth Cup hat trick against Norwich in December 2007.

BORN: March 15th 1983, Waterford.

SQUAD NUMBER: 14

FORMER CLUBS: Luton Town, Waterford, Sheffield Wednesday (loan).

FIVE FACTS ABOUT DARYL:

Republic of Ireland international.

Made his full international debut at the Giants Stadium in New York against Ecuador in 2007.

His goal against Wigan won the BBC TV Goal of the Month award for February 2008.

Scored 22 goals for Waterford in 2004.

2004 League of Ireland Young Player of the Year.

Forwards

Daryl Murphy

Nine of this line-up played in the 9-1 victory.

ALBERT MILTON
L.R. ROOSE
JOHN JOHNSTON
CHARLIE THOMPSON
HENRY FORSTER
TOMMY TAIT
HENRY LOW
GAVIN JARVIE
GEORGE HOLLEY
ARTHUR BRIDGETT
JACK
MORD
ARTHUR BROWN
BILLY HOGG

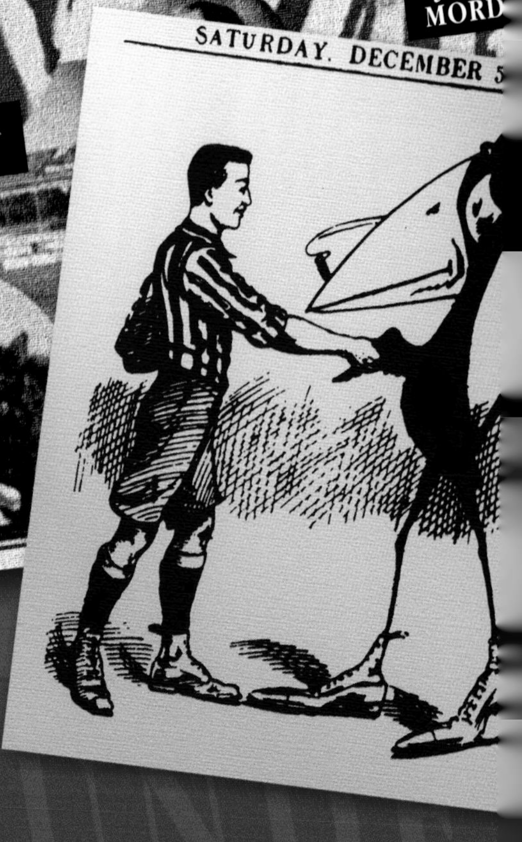

SATURDAY. DECEMBER 5

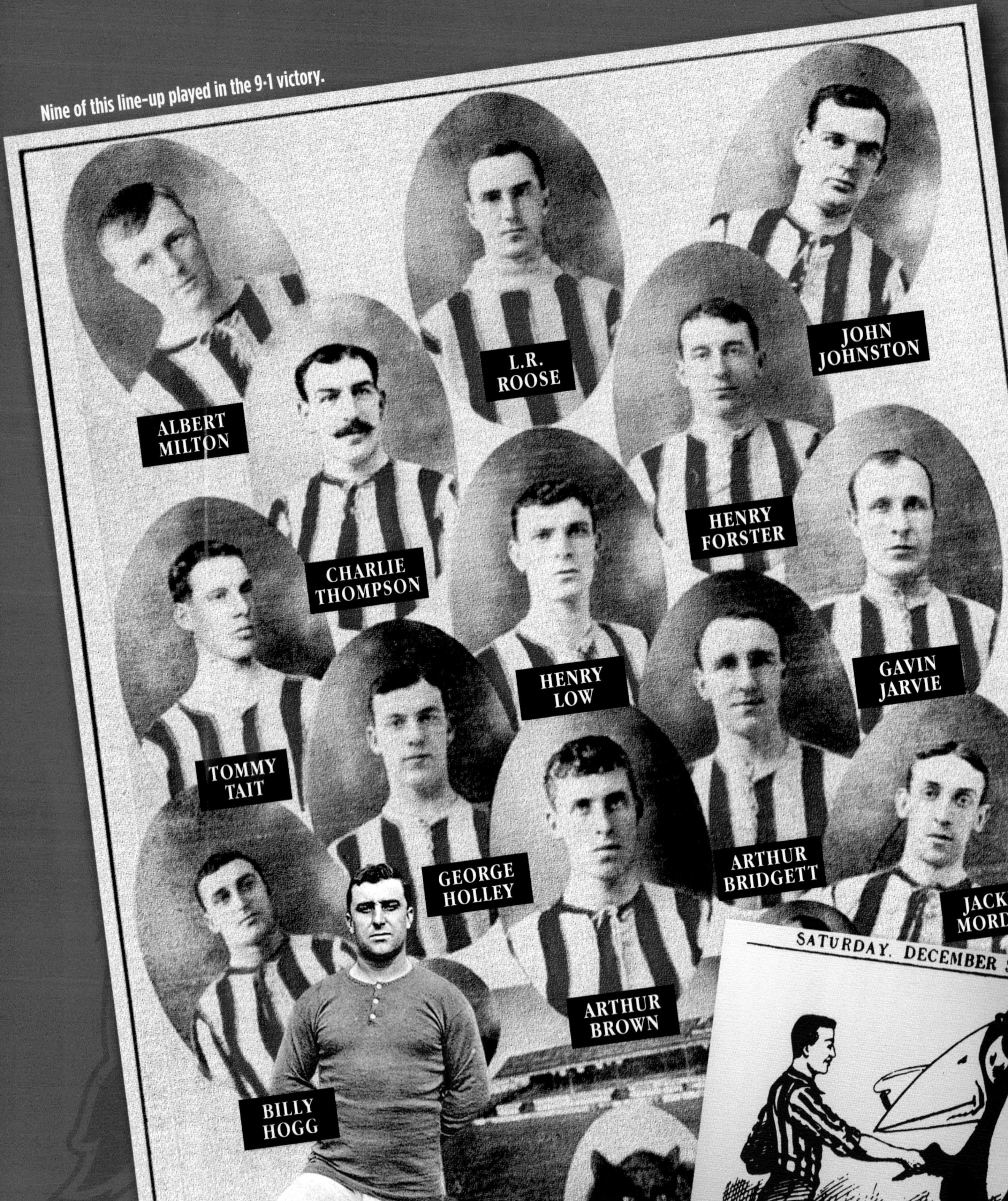

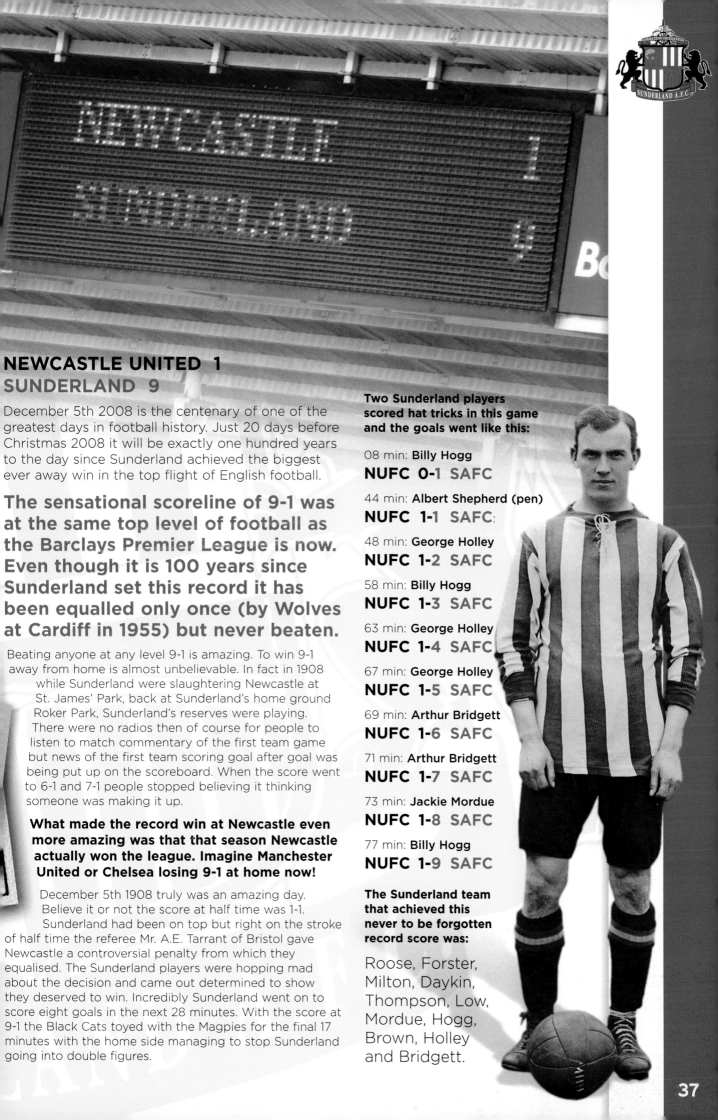

NEWCASTLE UNITED 1
SUNDERLAND 9

December 5th 2008 is the centenary of one of the greatest days in football history. Just 20 days before Christmas 2008 it will be exactly one hundred years to the day since Sunderland achieved the biggest ever away win in the top flight of English football.

The sensational scoreline of 9-1 was at the same top level of football as the Barclays Premier League is now. Even though it is 100 years since Sunderland set this record it has been equalled only once (by Wolves at Cardiff in 1955) but never beaten.

Beating anyone at any level 9-1 is amazing. To win 9-1 away from home is almost unbelievable. In fact in 1908 while Sunderland were slaughtering Newcastle at St. James' Park, back at Sunderland's home ground Roker Park, Sunderland's reserves were playing. There were no radios then of course for people to listen to match commentary of the first team game but news of the first team scoring goal after goal was being put up on the scoreboard. When the score went to 6-1 and 7-1 people stopped believing it thinking someone was making it up.

What made the record win at Newcastle even more amazing was that that season Newcastle actually won the league. Imagine Manchester United or Chelsea losing 9-1 at home now!

December 5th 1908 truly was an amazing day. Believe it or not the score at half time was 1-1. Sunderland had been on top but right on the stroke of half time the referee Mr. A.E. Tarrant of Bristol gave Newcastle a controversial penalty from which they equalised. The Sunderland players were hopping mad about the decision and came out determined to show they deserved to win. Incredibly Sunderland went on to score eight goals in the next 28 minutes. With the score at 9-1 the Black Cats toyed with the Magpies for the final 17 minutes with the home side managing to stop Sunderland going into double figures.

Two Sunderland players scored hat tricks in this game and the goals went like this:

08 min: **Billy Hogg**
NUFC 0-1 SAFC

44 min: **Albert Shepherd (pen)**
NUFC 1-1 SAFC:

48 min: **George Holley**
NUFC 1-2 SAFC

58 min: **Billy Hogg**
NUFC 1-3 SAFC

63 min: **George Holley**
NUFC 1-4 SAFC

67 min: **George Holley**
NUFC 1-5 SAFC

69 min: **Arthur Bridgett**
NUFC 1-6 SAFC

71 min: **Arthur Bridgett**
NUFC 1-7 SAFC

73 min: **Jackie Mordue**
NUFC 1-8 SAFC

77 min: **Billy Hogg**
NUFC 1-9 SAFC

The Sunderland team that achieved this never to be forgotten record score was:

Roose, Forster, Milton, Daykin, Thompson, Low, Mordue, Hogg, Brown, Holley and Bridgett.

Attendances in England are fantastic. Last season 29,914,212 watched games in the Barclays Premier League and the three divisions of the Football League. That's almost 30 million! It is the highest figure since 1967-68 when 30,107,298 attended games just two seasons after England won the World Cup.

Great

In the 2007-08 season Sunderland averaged

43,344

This was less than 200 under Liverpool and the 5th highest in the country.

Away from the Premier League both Leeds and Exeter also had their record attendances against SAFC

Sunderland are one of only three clubs to have been the visiting club for the record attendance of more than one other Premier League club.

The others are Arsenal and Derby

Hull City's record attendance of 55,019 against Man Utd was at their old Boothferry Park ground.

Their record attendance at their new KC Stadium was 25,512 against Sunderland in 2007.

Both Arsenal and Tottenham have their record attendances against

Sunderland

Grimsby Town have played in front of a bigger crowd than Man Utd ever have at Old Trafford!

United's biggest attendance of 76,096 is less then the 76,962 that watched Grimsby play Wolves at Old Trafford in an FA Cup semi final in 1939.

Gates

Sunderland's record attendance of

75,118

has been exceeded by only five other clubs.

Sunderland's record attendance of
75,118 is 6,732 higher
than any attendance ever achieved by any of the other north east clubs.

Nine of the teams in the FA Premier League (including Sunderland) had their record gates in FA Cup games.

CLUB	RECORD ATTENDANCE		
Arsenal	73,295	v Sunderland	1935
Aston Villa*	76,588	v Derby	1946
Blackburn Rovers*	62,522	v Bolton	1929
Bolton Wanderers*	69,912	v Man City	1933
Chelsea	82,905	v Arsenal	1935
Everton	78,299	v Liverpool	1948
Fulham	49,335	v Millwall	1938
Hull	55,019	v Man Utd	1949
Liverpool*	61,905	v Wolves	1952
Manchester City*	85,569	v Stoke	1934
Manchester Utd	76,098	v Blackburn	2007
Middlesbrough	53,536	v Newcastle	1949
Newcastle	68,386	v Chelsea	1930
Portsmouth*	51,385	v Derby	1949
Stoke	51,380	v Arsenal	1937
Sunderland*	75,118	v Derby	1933
Tottenham*	75,038	v Sunderland	1938
West Brom*	64,815	v Arsenal	1937
West Ham	42,322	v Tottenham	1970
Wigan	27,526	v Hereford	1953

*Record in an FA Cup tie

Young Professionals

Sunderland have some excellent young players almost all of whom were still to make their first team debuts at the start of this season but who are hoping to make the breakthrough into the first team. These players are...

JAMIE CHANDLER

BORN: March 24th 1989

POSITION: Centre / right midfield

SQUAD NUMBER: 38

England U19 international who always looks to play positively.

DAVID DOWSON

BORN: December 12th 1988

POSITION: Striker

SQUAD NUMBER: 40

Has been in England U18 squad.

A maker as well as a taker of goals.

JACK COLBACK

BORN: October 24th 1989

POSITION: Centre midfield

QUAD NUMBER: 34

Former captain of the U18 team. Played for the first team in pre-season against Cobh Ramblers.

PETER HARTLEY

BORN: April 3rd 1988

POSITION: Centre back / left back

SQUAD NUMBER: 29

Played seven minutes for the first team at Leicester on New Year Day 2007. Gained league experien on loan to Chesterfield in 2008.

JORDAN COOK

BORN: March 20th 1990

POSITION: Almost anywhere!

Versatile player from Easington Lane who has played up front, in midfield and at right back.

JORDAN HENDERSON

BORN: June 6th 1990

POSITION: Midfield

SQUAD NUMBER: 42

Talented creative midfielder with the ability to score from long distance. Played for the first tea against Ajax in pre-season.

CONOR
HOURIHANE

BORN: February 2nd 1991

POSITION: Midfield

SQUAD NUMBER: 43

Highly rated Republic of Ireland junior international. Played for the first team in a Testimonial at Falkirk last season.

NIALL
McARDLE

BORN: March 22nd 1990

POSITION: Centre back

Republic of Ireland U18 international from Malahide.

MICHAEL
KAY

BORN: September 19th 1989

POSITION: Right back

SQUAD NUMBER: 35

England youth international. On the bench for a Premier League match at Man Utd in September 2007.

DAVID
MEYLER

BORN: May 25th 1989

POSITION: Midfield

SQUAD NUMBER: 41

Signed from Cork City in summer 2008. Three senior games for Cork. Played for SAFC first team against Cobh Ramblers in pre-season.

MICHAEL
LIDDLE

BORN: December 25th 1989

POSITION: Left back

SQUAD NUMBER: 33

Already a Republic of Ireland U21 international, Michael celebrates his birthday on Christmas Day.

JEAN YVES
M'VOTO

BORN: September 6th 1988

POSITION: Centre back

SQUAD NUMBER: 25

Big, powerful defender signed from Paris St. Germain.

NATHAN
LUSCOMBE

BORN: November 6th 1989

POSITION: Left midfield/back

SQUAD NUMBER: 36

Exciting player who top scored for the U18s in the league in 07-08 with 17 goals. Played for the first team three times in pre-season including the match with Ajax.

ROBBIE
WEIR

BORN: December 12th 1988

POSITION: Midfield/right back

SQUAD NUMBER: 37

Northern Ireland U21 international and U18s captain from 2006-07. A versatile player.

Martyn Waghorn from this group is featured on pages 34-35.

CUP TRAIL

Can you help Sunderland to win the FA Cup? Not since Bob Stokoe's legendary team of 1973 have the lads managed to win the world's oldest football competition. The FA Cup actually starts in August with non league teams battling their way through qualifying rounds to get into the first round which is the point that teams from the Football League enter.

Sunderland and the rest of the Premier League and Championship teams come into the competition at the third round stage in early January. There are then fourth and fifth rounds before the quarter final and semi final stage leading up to the Wembley final which in 2009 will take place on May 30th. The winners of the FA Cup qualify for the UEFA Cup.

PLAY THE GAME

- **You will need a dice and counters for each player.**
- **You must throw a three to start.**

Once you have thrown a three, have another throw and whatever number you get is the number of squares you can move. After that every time it is your turn throw the dice and move your counter as many squares as you get on your roll of the dice unless you come up to a cup round in which case you must stop on that square and play the game. You always need some luck to win the cup,

so good luck!

13
You've reached Round Four and you are drawn at home to Sheffield Wednesday.
FOLLOW THE CUP ACTION INSTRUCTIONS

14
You've got a tough draw in the next round of the cup, take one off your score when you roll your dice for your score in the fifth round game.

El-Hadji Diouf picks up an injury
MISS A TURN

1
It's 0-0 early on.
STAY WHERE YOU ARE

12
You make a major new signing.
ADD ONE TO YOUR SCORE WHEN YOU ROLL THE DICE FOR YOUR FOURTH ROUND MATCH.

2
You've got a corner.
HAVE ANOTHER TURN

11
You lose an important league game.
MISS A TURN

3
The opposition have a corner and you need to defend it.
MISS A TURN

10

Your right back commits a bad foul in a league game and gets a red card
MISS A TURN

4

9
You've got injury problems after your third round match.
MISS A TURN

5

6
It's the day before the third round and you are all excited.
MOVE TO SQUARE SEVEN

7
You've reached Round Three and you are drawn away to Hartlepool.
FOLLOW THE CUP ACTION INSTRUCTIONS
SEE BOTTOM OF PAGE 43

8
The draw for the fourth round is a good one for you.
HAVE AN EXTRA TURN

You are on square 37 and Sunderland won the cup in 1973, but you are playing Liverpool who beat Sunderland in the 1992 final. Which way will it go?

26

27

28
You've reached the Quarter Final and you are drawn at home to Man City.
FOLLOW THE CUP ACTION INSTRUCTIONS

25
Some of your injury problems clear up.
MOVE ON TO THE NEXT SQUARE

29
You are delighted to have beaten Man City after their win at the Stadium of Light earlier this league season.
GO STRAIGHT TO SEMI FINAL, SQUARE 34

37
You've reached the Final and you are playing Liverpool at Wembley.
FOLLOW THE CUP ACTION INSTRUCTIONS

24

30

36
Cup fever grips Sunderland.
GO TO THE FINAL SQUARE

23
Everyone is thrilled to have beaten Spurs.
TAKE AN EXTRA TURN

31

35

22
You've reached Round Five and you are drawn away to Spurs.
FOLLOW THE CUP ACTION INSTRUCTIONS

32
Craig Gordon is doubtful for the semi final.
MISS A TURN

33

34
You've reached the Semi Final and you are drawn against Arsenal at the neutral venue of Villa Park.
FOLLOW THE CUP ACTION INSTRUCTIONS

20
of your players are late raining and you decide teach them a lesson.
MISS TWO TURNS

21

CUP ACTION

Whenever you reach a square that is a cup round (red squares) you must stop on that square even if you were only two squares off it and have rolled a six. You cannot go past a cup round square unless you've played that game and won it.

When you reach a cup round square this is what you have to do to find the score of your game:

- **Let the player to your right roll the dice for your opponents' score.**
- **Roll the dice for your score.**
- **Whatever the two rolls of the dice are is the result. If you've won keep going, if you've lost you're out of the cup and your game is over already.**

If you both have the same score, roll again to see what the 'replay' score is.

If the scores are still level then it is penalties: have five rolls of the dice each and add up your total score – highest stays in the cup. If the score is still level keep taking turns having one roll of the dice each until there is a winner!

RED, WHITE & Pr

ud!

Sunderland supporters are amongst the most passionate in the land. Sunderland's junior supporters club is called 24-7 due to the fact that Sunderland fans live and breathe SAFC twenty four hours a day, seven days a week.

What is going on at the club, who Sunderland might be signing, selling or loaning is never far from supporters' minds. News of how those players recovering from injury are progressing is latched upon and everyone will have an opinion - usually a strong one - about each and every player.

What all this means is that on Wearside football matters. To many it matters more than just about anything else. Obviously people should care for their family first and foremost but that's one of the ways that the match comes in. People lead busy lives, always dashing about from here to there and often not making the time they'd like to see brothers, sisters and so on but once the match at the Stadium of Light beckons that is the opportunity to families who might live some miles apart to meet up, catch up on some gossip and roar on the red and whites.

In 2008 a study of every Premier League ground recording decibel levels examined which crowd made the most noise and for the longest periods.

Guess which fans made the most noise? You are looking at them!

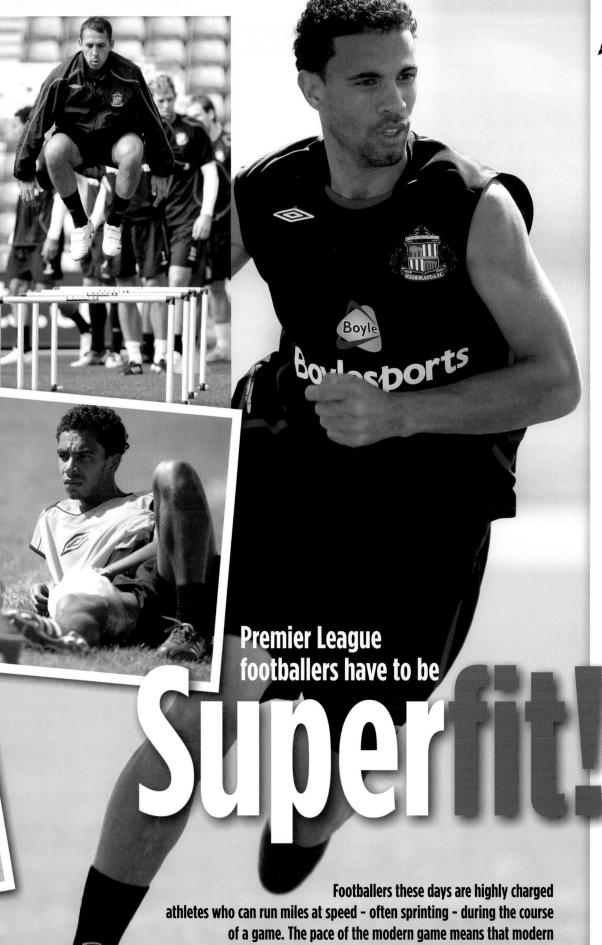

Premier League footballers have to be Superfit!

Footballers these days are highly charged athletes who can run miles at speed - often sprinting - during the course of a game. The pace of the modern game means that modern footballers have to maintain an exceptionally high level of fitness.

At Sunderland, Roy Keane's back room staff include people dedicated to working on strength and conditioning in addition to people who do the actual football coaching. If you ever get the chance to see the players train then do so and you'll gain an idea of how hard footballers have to work to make sure they're in tip-top condition for when the match is on.

It is a global game and these days whenever there's an international break SAFC's squad jet off across the world.

With Dwight Yorke, Carlos Edwards and Kenwyne Jones involved in Trinidad and Tobago's World Cup campaign any of that trio can have a long trans-Atlantic flight for a game while El-Hadji Diouf is one of the biggest names in Africa - in fact he has been African Footballer of the Year twice! El-Hadji plays for Senegal and is a star of their team.

Djibril Cisse stars for France for whom Pascal Chimbonda has also played although Steed Malbranque went into this season still awaiting a full cap although he has played for France at U21 level.

Kieran Richardson scored twice on his England debut against the USA and if he can consistently show his best form he is capable of featuring in Fabio Capello's plans for the future. North of the border Craig Gordon is Scotland's number one as well as Sunderland's. Craig is one of four full international goalies at Sunderland with Marton Fulop (Hungary), Darren Ward (Wales) and Nick Colgan (Republic of Ireland) all having full international experience.

Sunderland of course have a host of Republic of Ireland internationals as well as former Republic internationals as chairman and manager while north of the Irish border David Healy is a legend in his international shirt and was even the top scorer in Europe during his country's qualification games for Euro 2008!

Daryl Murphy
Republic of Ireland

Marton Fulop · Hungary

Graham Kavanagh · Republic of Ireland

Pascal Chimbonda · France

Anthony Stokes
Republic of Ireland

David Connolly
Republic of Ireland

Kieran Richardson · England

Carlos Edwards
Trinidad & Tobago

Rade Prica
Sweden

Dwight Yorke
Trinidad & Tobago

International Stars

David Healy
Northern Ireland

Andy Reid
Republic of Ireland

Kenwyne Jones
Trinidad & Tobago

Craig Gordon · Scotland

McShane
ublic of Ireland

Teemu Tainio · Finland

Darren Ward · Wales

Danny Collins · Wales

Djibril Cisse · France

Nick Colgan
Republic of Ireland

Liam Miller
Republic
of Ireland

er-Hadji Diouf · Senegal

30 things you didn't know about

Sunderland

Sunderland is a great place with lots going for it as well as a Premier League football club.

How many of these facts surprise you?

01 The Stadium of Light is the magnificent home of Sunderland AFC, widely regarded as one of the best stadia in Europe. Standing on the banks of the River Wear the stadium's design drew inspiration from Sunderland's proud industrial heritage in glass making, shipbuilding and coal mining.

02 Sunderland is one of the world's seven most IT intelligent communities. Sunderland has been awarded a lifetime achievement for its digital know-how at the IT Intelligent Community Awards in New York.

03 Perhaps Sunderland's most prominent landmark is Penshaw Monument - it even appears on SAFC's club badge. It was built in 1844 in honour of the first Earl of Durham, John George Lambton. Penshaw was modelled on the Theseion, the Temple of Theseus in Athens. It stands magnificently above the city on a limestone hill in the middle of the Great North Forest and can be seen as far away as Durham Cathedral and the North Pennines.

04 Sunderland is the largest city in the North East of England, with almost 300,000 residents and more than two million people living within a 30 minute radius.

05 The twin churches and monastery sites of St Peter's, Sunderland and St Paul's, Jarrow is the UK's nomination for UNESCO World Heritage Site 2010. The monasteries were the home to the author of the first history of England, the Venerable Bede.

06 Sunderland has gained a worldwide reputation as a centre for making cars, employing 12,000 people in the sector.

07 Sunderland's Aquatic Centre is the region's only 50-metre swimming pool between Leeds and Edinburgh. The flagship pool is a £20 milli project. It is next to the Stadium of Light and there are high hopes that it will be used as a training facility for the 2012 Olympics.

08 In a study, Sunderland was ranked in the top five of the most competitive locations that companies like to do business with.

09 Sunderland has signed a Friendship Agreement with Washington DC which makes Sunderland the only city in Europe to enjoy such a relations with the world's most powerful city. Washington Old Hall is home to the direct ancestors of the first president of the United States of America.

10 Sunderland is one of the few cities in the UK to have a river and beautiful coastline. Both beaches at Roker and Seaburn are Blue Flag Beaches.

11 The Sunderland International Airshow is the biggest free airshow in Europe and has been going for 20 years.

12 Sunderland marks the easterly end of the 140-mile C2C (Coast to Coast) route. The C2C cycle trail from Whitehaven in Cumbria to Sunderland is Britain's most popular long distance cycle route, with between 12,000 and 15,000 cyclists completing it every year.

13 Sunderland-born DJ and ex-Kenicke singer Lauren Laverne is a TV star brimming with Northern attitude and can be seen hosting The Culture Show.

14 Sunderland was voted the most giving city in the UK in a poll for The Giving Campaign, a partnership between the Government and the charity sector.

15 Sunderland Museum and Winter Gardens is officially the best large visitor attraction outside London. It is free and has been awarded the second place in the Large Visitor Attraction category, Excellence in England awards.

16 Blockbuster West End shows including Miss Saigon and Starlight Express, have been staged at the Sunderland Empire, the biggest theatre between Edinburgh and Manchester.

17 Joseph Swan, who invented the electric light bulb independently of Thomas Edison, was born in 1828 at Pallion Hall, Sunderland. He also invented artificial silk, bromide photographic paper, the lead storage battery and the carbon printing process.

18 The New Musical Express, or NME as it is universally known, has named Sunderland one of the coolest places for underground music. It is home to the Futureheads.

19 The fascinating new facsimile of the Lindisfarne Gospels is available to view at Sunderland's City Library and Arts Centre.

20 The tranquil haven of Mowbray Park in Sunderland City Centre is one of the oldest municipal parks in the North East. Now restored to its former Victorian splendour, it has an intriguing array of art works celebrating the city's connection with Lewis Carroll who wrote his famous poem Jabberwocky whilst staying in the city.

21 The University of Sunderland's new Media Centre is at the forefront of UK teaching and research in TV, radio, video & new media production, journalism, PR, film, media and cultural studies. Former University Chancellor – Oscar winning film producer Lord Puttnam - said it is 'a wonderful example of Sunderland being able to offer its region and its students the very, very best there is'.

22 Home of The National Glass Centre the only UK centre celebrating the history of glass making and providing a world focus for glass making.

23 Park Lane Interchange, Sunderland is the second most used bus station in the country after London Victoria.

24 The Sunderland International Festival of Kites, Music and Dance is the biggest event of its kind in the country.

25 Sunderland is the home to a collection of LS Lowry paintings, England's best loved artist. Lowry thought of Sunderland as his second home.

26 One of the oldest windmills and best preserved relics of Britain's industrial heritage is Fulwell Mill, a Grade 11 listed building dating from 1821.

27 James Herriot, the man responsible for an entire generation wanting to become vets was born in Sunderland as James Alfred Wight on October 3 1916 and was a huge Sunderland supporter. The Stadium of Light has a James Herriott Suite.

28 Other celebrities who can claim a Wearside pedigree are newscaster Kate Adie, Dave Stewart from Eurthymics, actor James Bolam, cricketer Bob Willis, Charles Alcock, the founder of the FA Cup and Frank Wilson. Frank Wilson became Prime Minister of Australia in the years before WW1 and is proof that Wearsiders are destined to go far.

Frank Wilson

29 Sunderland has produced a pope - almost! History records Nicholas Breakspear (Adrian IV) as the only English pope but in the 14th Century the Great Schism produced two rival pontiffs. The legitimate line was supported by the French but there was a succession of antipopes backed by the Holy Roman Emperor. The first antipope, named Clement VII, was Robert of Geneva who, before his elevation, served as a Wearmouth parish priest.

30 Sunderland has the premier artificial indoor climbing wall climbing wall in Europe.

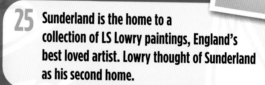

SUNDERLAND A.F.C.

Academy Players

Sunderland have one of the most highly regarded Academy set ups in the country. Academy manager Ged McNamee, assisted by Kevin Ball and Elliott Dickman look to nurture young talent and feed players through to the young reserve side for what is known in the club as the Development squad.

The U18 team have won their league for the last two seasons and last year reached the semi finals of the FA Youth Cup. This year's squad is mainly made up of new players although several of the second years played important roles in the 07-08 season's success.

First Years

MATTHEW FLETCHER

BORN: May 12th 1992

POSITION: Forward

Australian born forward who created both goals in the first win of the 2008-09 season at West Brom.

NATHAN WILSON

BORN: March 2nd 1992

POSITION: Midfield

Darlington born player who has been with Sunderland since he was a member of the U9 team.

BLAIR ADAMS

BORN: September 8th 1991

POSITION: Left back

South Shields lad once with Newcastle. Played at the Stadium of Light in the FA Youth Cup in December 2007.

CRAIG LYNCH

BORN: March 25th 1992

POSITION: Midfield

Technically gifted player from Bowburn who has worked his way up through the age groups at SAFC.

BEN WILSON

BORN: August 9th 1992

POSITION: Goalkeep

The youngest memb the year group and a the club since the U11 year. From Edmondsl in Durham.

LIAM BAGNALL

BORN: Born May 17th 1992

POSITION: Right back / midfield

Northern Ireland U16 captain and U17 international. Competitive player from Newry.

RYAN NOBLE

BORN: November 6th 1991

POSITION: Forward

Top scorer for the U16s in 2007-08 when he also got a couple of goals in the U18s FA Youth Cup side. Sunderland born.

BEN WOOD

BORN: October 9th 1991

POSITION: Striker/ midfield

Intelligent player who h been called into Englan training camps. Scored first U18 goal in the firs of the 2008-09 season West Brom.

Second Years

LIAM **HUBBOCK**

BORN: February 2nd 1991

POSITION: Forward

Former Wallsend Boys Club player who missed most of his first year through injury.

LIAM **NOBLE**

BORN: May 8th 1991

POSITION: Midfield

Former Wallsend Boys Club player who became more and more involved in his first year and is now a key player. Good passer and reader of the game.

DAVID **BROWN**

BORN: February 19th 1991

POSITION: Central defender/left back

England youth international from Stanley.

MARTIN **HUNTER**

BORN: September 16th 1990

POSITION: Goalkeeper

Whitley Bay lad who made his debut at Ninian Park Cardiff in the FA Youth Cup in 07.

ADAM **REED**

BORN: May 8th 1991

POSITION: Midfield

Saw his first year hampered by injury. Hartlepool lad who scored a screamer at the Stadium of Light v Norwich in the FA Youth Cup.

JOE **CORNFORTH**

BORN: December 28th 1990

POSITION: Central defender

Nephew of former SAFC player John Cornforth. Scored a terrific goal in the FA Youth Cup to knock holders Liverpool out in 2008.

DAN **MADDEN**

BORN: September 10th 1990

POSITION: Central defender

Captain of the U18s, powerful centre half who was injured for almost all of his first season.

GAVIN **SCOTT**

Born: December 12th 1990

POSITION: Winger

Hailing from Southmoor in Stanley, Gavin has been with SAFC since the U14 age group.

ANDREW **GALER**

BORN: September 19th 1990

POSITION: Forward

Sunderland born forward who first played for the U18s when he was still 15.

MICHAL **MISIEWICZ**

BORN: October 11th 1990

POSITION: Goalkeeper

Polish / Canadian 'keeper who represents Canada. Signed from Plymouth Argyle.

ADAM **SLEGG**

BORN: Born October 5th 1990

POSITION: Winger

Impressed when playing against SAFC for Kent Academy in summer 2007 and taken on.

Conor Hourihane is a second year who already has a first team squad number so see pages 40-41.

STEED
Malbranque

KIERAN
Richardson

Dean Whitehead: Led Sunderland to the 2007 Championship and was joint North east Footballer of the Year that year.

SAFC Skippers

Being captain of the team is an important job. It involves a lot more than simply wearing the captain's armband and calling a side of the coin at the toss up. Some captains simply try to lead by example.

Dean Whitehead for instance tries to lead by always showing absolute commitment from the first whistle to the last. Other skippers lead by constantly talking to their team mates, maybe even involving a bit of fist shaking when necessary, Kevin Ball who captained the team for most of the 1990s was this sort of skipper.

Sunderland have had some great captains over the years and we pick some of them out here.

Stan Anderson: England international midfielder who led Sunderland before Hurley.

Kevin Ball: Captained the team to the Championship in 1996 and also 1999 when leading the team to a record 105 points.

Raich Carter: All time England great who skippered and scored for the club's first FA Cup winners in 1937.

Barry Venison: The youngest ever Wembley captain when he skippered Sunderland in the 1985 League Cup final in the absence of the suspended Shaun Elliott.

Charlie Hurley: SAFC's Player of the Century who captained the club's first ever promotion team of 1964.

Bobby Kerr: the 'Little General' who captained the 1973 FA Cup winning team.

Alex Hastings: captained the side for most of the 1936 title win although Carter captained the team on the day the league was clinched.

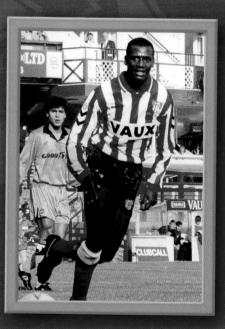

Rob Hindmarch: Sunderland's youngest ever captain when he led the team out at Nottingham Forest in December 1980 when he was just 19 years and 247 days old.

Gary Bennett: Captained the team to two promotions in the late 80s and early 90s.

Great Goals

Sunderland's first win of this season away to Tottenham featured two fabulous goals: Kieran Richardson's screamer and Djibril Cisse's header set a high standard to keep up. There have been some spectacular Sunderland goals in the last couple of years. Can you remember these?

Daryl Murphy's BBC TV Goal of the Month winner against Wigan last season when he lashed home a 30 yarder after picking up a superb crossfield pass from Andy Reid.

Michael Chopra's late winner away to Aston Villa in March.

Carlos Edwards' wonder goal against Burnley in the last home game as promotion was won in 2007 or the same player's brilliant goals away to Birmingham and Southampton during the same season.

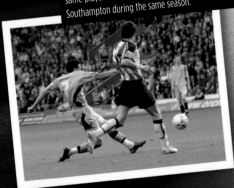

Liam Miller's left foot screamer away to 'Boro in September 2007.

Kenwyne Jones' towering header away to Arsenal in 2007.

Both of Kieran Richardson's well taken goals in the 2-0 win over Portsmouth in January 2008.

Danny Higginbotham's header v Newcastle last season.

at are YOUR favourite goals?

est goal I've ever seen Sunderland score was scored by:

_____

est goal I've ever seen any team score was scored by:

_____

_____

_____

inst:

_____

e best goal I've ever scored was when I...

_____

_____

_____

_____

_____

_____

_____

FA CUP WINNERS '73

1937

2005

Cup final

Sunderland have been in four FA Cup finals, winning in 1973 and 1937. In 1913 they won the league and reached the FA Cup final where they lost 1-0 to Aston Villa before a crowd of 120,000, the second highest crowd ever in England behind the attendance for the first ever FA Cup final at Wembley ten years later. Sunderland were most recently in the FA Cup final in 1992 when they lost 2-0 to Liverpool.

In 1973 Sunderland famously won one of the most famous FA Cup finals ever. Up against Leeds United who at that time were one of the top sides in Europe Sunderland won 1-0 with a goal by Ian Porterfield. What made the final even more unforgettable was the double save goalkeeper Jim Montgomery made from Leeds' Trevor Cherry and Peter Lorimer which is the most famous save ever made in any game at the national stadium.

Sunderland's first FA Cup win had been when the numbers seven and three came the other way round: 1937. At that time Sunderland had a brilliant team with great players such as Raich Carter, Jimmy Connor, Patsy Gallacher and Bobby Gurney. They beat Preston North End 3-1 in the final just a year after Sunderland had won the league title. Sunderland have been in a dozen semi-finals, most recently in 2004.

1999 SAFC Records

CHAMPIONS 2007 SUNDERLAND A.F.C.

Only five teams (Liverpool, Man Utd., Arsenal. Everton and Aston Villa) have been champions of England more times than Sunderland who have been champions six times. Until 1992-93 the trophy now used for what is currently known as the Championship was used for the winners of the top level of English football. It was only after the creation of the FA Premier League that this trophy started to be used for winning the second level of English football.

Sunderland were champions of England three times in the first decade of the Football League establishing Sunderland as one of the country's leading clubs right at the beginning of league football in the 1890s. The Lads added further titles in 1902, 1913 and 1936.

Football League Cup

Sunderland have yet to win the Football League Cup. The nearest they got to it was in 1985 when Len Ashurst's side lost 1-0 in the final to Norwich City. A great cup run that had included beating Spurs at White Hart Lane and a 5-2 aggregate win over Chelsea in the semi final, ended at Wembley where Clive Walker hit the post with a penalty for Sunderland who were beaten 1-0 when a shot deflected in off centre half Gordon Chisholm for an own goal. The club were also semi finalists in 1963 and 1999.

BIGGEST WIN:
11-1 v Fairfield FA Cup 1st round
February 2nd 1895

BIGGEST LEAGUE WIN:
Newcastle United 1-9, Sunderland, 5.12.1908 (This has never been beaten by any away side in top flight football)

HIGHEST SCORING DRAW:
5-5 v Liverpool (h) 19.1.1907
& v Middlesbrough (a) 17.10.1936

CONSECUTIVE WINS:
13, November 14th 1891 to April 2nd 1892

CONSECUTIVE HOME WINS:
19, December 20th 1890 to 16th April 1892

CONSECUTIVE UNBEATEN HOME RECORD:
44 games
October 18th 1890 to December 6th 1893.

MOST POINTS IN A SEASON:
105 points 1998-99

MOST WINS IN A SEASON:
31, 1998-99

MOST DRAWS IN A SEASON:
18, 1954-55 & 1994-95

MOST LEAGUE GOALS SCORED IN A SEASON:
109, 1935-36

SUNDERLAND WERE THE FIRST TEAM TO EVER SCORE 100 GOALS IN A SEASON:
1892-93

1999

YOUNGEST EVER PLAYER:
Derek Forster, 15 years & 185 days when he played in goal in the top flight against Leicester on August 22nd 1964

OLDEST EVER PLAYER:
Thomas Urwin, 39 years & 76 days v Preston April 22nd 1935

MOST APPEARANCES:
627 Jim Montgomery 1961 to 1976. This figure includes 12 games in the Anglo-Italian, Anglo-Scottish and Texaco cups which while in minor competitions were competitive games.

MOST GOALS:
228 Bobby Gurney, 1925-46

MOST LEAGUE GOALS:
209, Charlie Buchan, 1911 - 1925

MOST GOALS IN A SEASON:
43, Dave Halliday, 1928-29

HIGHEST ATTENDANCE:
75,118 v Derby County, FA Cup, March 8th 1933

ANSWERS

PAGE 14: HOW HIGH CAN YOU GO?

01. El-Hadji Diouf
02. Djibril Cisse
03. Daryl Murphy
04. Grant Leadbitter
05. Phil Bardsley
06. Danny Collins
07. Nyron Nosworthy and Dean Whitehead
08. Anton Ferdinand and George McCartney
09. Gretna
10. Michael Chopra
11. David Healy
12. Darren Ward
13. Senegal
14. Pascal Chimbonda
15. Carlos Edwards
16. Steed Malbranque
17. Andy Reid, Michael Chopra and Darren Ward
18. Sheffield Wednesday
19. Finland
20. Kieran Richardson
21. Republic of Ireland
22. Marytn Waghorn
23. El-Hadji Diouf
24. Dwight Yorke
25. David Healy
26. 2003
27. All are on season long loans
28. Pascal Chimbonda
29. Danny Collins
30. Djibril Cisse
31. Belgium
32. Nyron Nosworthy
33. Dwight Yorke
34. Phil Bardsley
35. Kenwyne Jones
36. Daryl Murphy
37. Andy Reid
38. El-Hadji Diouf, Djibril Cisse, Dwight Yorke, Carlos Edwards and Kenwyne Jones

PAGE 33: WHO AM I?

A. Andy Reid
B. Steed Malbranque
C. Dwight Yorke

PAGE 33: SPOT THE DIFFERENCE